essential careers™

A CAREER AS A
PLUMBER

SIMONE PAYMENT

ROSEN
PUBLISHING

NEW YORK

The author would like to thank Casey Connell
for his time and help with background information.

Published in 2011 by The Rosen Publishing Group, Inc.
29 East 21st Street, New York, NY 10010

Library of Congress Cataloging-in-Publication Data

Payment, Simone.
A career as a plumber / Simone Payment.—1st ed.
    p. cm.—(Essential careers)
Includes bibliographical references and index.
ISBN 978-1-4358-9473-0 (library binding)
1. Plumbing—Juvenile literature. 2. Plumbers—Vocational guidance—Juvenile literature. I. Title.
TH6124.P39 2011
696'.1023—dc22

                                                                    2009043664

Manufactured in the United States of America

CPSIA Compliance Information: Batch #S10YA: For Further Information Contact Rosen Publishing, New York, New York at 1-800-237-9932

contents

INTRODUCTION 4

CHAPTER 1: WHAT DOES A PLUMBER DO? 8

CHAPTER 2: RELATED CAREERS 16

CHAPTER 3: PREPARING TO BE A PLUMBER 24

CHAPTER 4: APPRENTICESHIP PROGRAMS 32

CHAPTER 5: WORKING AS A PLUMBER 39

CHAPTER 6: GETTING A LICENSE

AND BEGINNING A CAREER 54

GLOSSARY 68

FOR MORE INFORMATION 70

FOR FURTHER READING 74

BIBLIOGRAPHY 75

INDEX 77

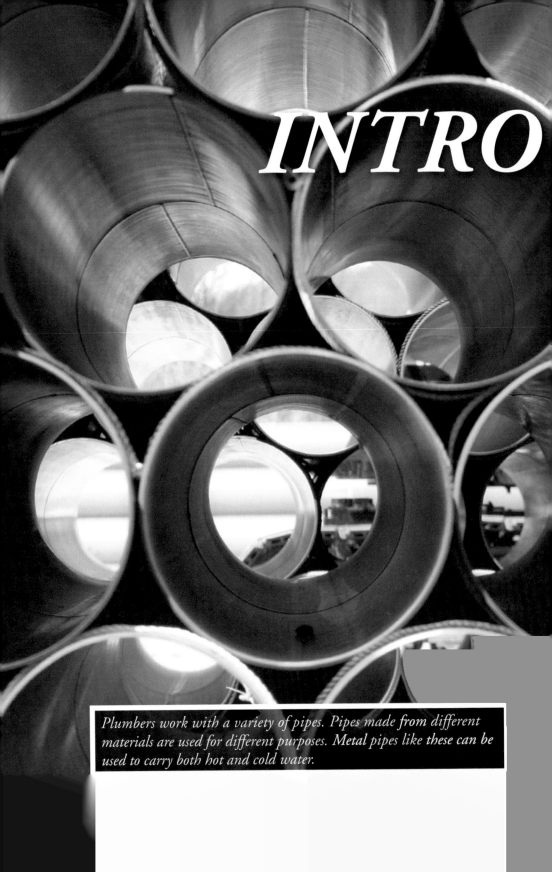

INTRO

Plumbers work with a variety of pipes. Pipes made from different materials are used for different purposes. Metal pipes like these can be used to carry both hot and cold water.

DUCTION

S ome careers are closely linked to the national economy. When the economy is strong, there are many jobs available in those careers. When times are tough, there are not. During difficult economic times, people who work in these careers may have their work hours reduced, and therefore make less money. Businesses may even begin cutting back on their staff.

For example, careers in the food service industry are closely linked to the performance of the national economy. During good economic times, many people have disposable income and are more likely to go out to eat. As a result, it is easy for job seekers to find work in the food service industry. When the economy is bad, however, not as many people can afford to eat at restaurants. Jobs as cooks or servers become harder to find, and restaurant workers may work fewer hours, or earn less money in tips.

Other careers are less affected by recessions and economic downturns. No matter what the state of the economy, there are certain services that people simply cannot do without.

Plumbers perform tasks that every household needs. They install household fixtures such as sinks, bathtubs, and washing machines; fix leaky pipes and clogged drains; install systems of pipes in buildings; and connect buildings to sewer or septic systems. Since virtually every building, from small houses to huge hospitals, has pipes, plumbers will always be needed.

When the economy is bad, people might choose to save money by putting off building a new home. However, it is unlikely that they'll wait to fix a broken sink. They may choose to remodel their current home instead of buying or building a new home. Some people may want to install green plumbing systems to conserve resources and save money. During a slow economy, plumbers may lose a little business, but they will usually have enough work doing repairs or remodeling. Cliff Brookes, a plumber in New Jersey, told the *New York Times* that most of his business during hard economic times is repairs or emergencies. According to Brookes, "Plumbers are lucky because people at least have things that need to be fixed all the time."

Becoming a plumber can be a good career choice for people who want to have more job security during hard economic times. There is no guarantee that a plumber will keep his or her job when times are tough—even plumbers can be laid off from their jobs. However, there are many other reasons why plumbing is a good career choice in any kind of economy. In the coming years, many plumbers will be retiring. According to the U.S. Bureau of Labor Statistics, fewer and fewer people have chosen to become plumbers over the past couple of decades. As existing plumbers retire, there will be fewer people to fill their positions. This will make it easier for aspiring plumbers to find a job.

Plumbers may also have more work in the coming years as people update their current plumbing systems to make them more "green," or environmentally friendly. Scientists believe that human activity has contributed to climate change, warming our planet and causing changes to Earth's environment. In addition, the price of energy keeps going up. Many people are trying to conserve energy and save natural resources like water. Plumbers can help with this effort by installing energy-efficient plumbing. For example, plumbers might replace existing bathroom fixtures with low-flow toilets and showerheads. They can also create systems to reuse water from dishwashers, washing machines, and showers. These are called gray water systems. Plumbers can also install tankless water heaters that save energy.

Another advantage of being a plumber is that plumbers can find work anywhere. A career as a plumber can be a good option for people who don't want to be tied down to one particular location for their work. People who want to move to a new state or country can usually get a job as a plumber, although they may need to learn about plumbing codes specific to their new location.

Being a plumber is an excellent career choice for someone who enjoys making things or doing physical labor. Plumbing can provide a great sense of accomplishment. Once plumbers are finished with a project, they can take pride in having created something useful.

chapter 1

WHAT DOES A PLUMBER DO?

Without plumbers, people wouldn't be able to enjoy many of the conveniences of modern living. Want a cold glass of water on a hot day? A plumber hooked up the kitchen faucet. Ready for a hot bath on a winter night? A plumber installed the water heater that warms the water that will fill the bathtub. They installed the dishwashers in a school cafeteria and the washing machines at the local laundromat. Although we take these conveniences for granted, they would not be available to us without the efforts of professional plumbers.

Some plumbers choose to focus on a particular kind of plumbing or pursue related careers. For instance, some plumbers choose to become pipe fitters, pipe layers, steamfitters, or sprinkler fitters. These jobs will be discussed in the next chapter.

GENERAL STATISTICS

According to the Bureau of Labor Statistics, there are more than half a million pipe fitters, pipe layers, plumbers, steamfitters, and sprinkler fitters in the United States. About half of them work for contractors. Plumbers that work for contractors may install plumbing in new homes or buildings, or they might

This plumber has brought his tools to the job site, where he is installing a sink. It is common for licensed plumbers to work in both private homes and commercial buildings.

WHAT IS A UNION?

A union is a group of workers in the same profession that come together to improve their working situation. For example, teachers or carpenters might form a union. Unions are also sometimes referred to as labor unions or trade unions. Unions try to increase workers' wages or benefits, such as health insurance and retirement plans. Unions also work toward making safety improvements in the industry. They can also help union members if they have problems with an employer.

In North America, many plumbers belong to the United Association of Journeymen and Apprentices of the Plumbing and Pipe Fitting Industry of the United States and Canada. This union, which is also known as the UA, is made up of about three hundred smaller local unions. Although plumbers are not usually required to join a union, many find that membership in the UA is beneficial.

fix or update existing plumbing. Other plumbers work outside of the construction industry. For example, they might work on a natural gas pipeline or for the oil industry. About 10 percent of all plumbers work for themselves, rather than for a company. About one-third of plumbers belong to a union.

In general, plumbers make the highest salary of all the jobs in the construction industry. Of course, not all plumbers make the same salary. Their pay can vary depending on where they work, the tasks they perform, and their level of expertise. For a list of current plumbing salaries, refer to the Bureau of Labor Statistics' *Occupational Outlook Handbook* (http://www.bls.gov/oco).

TYPES OF JOBS

Many plumbers work on new construction projects. Some work on residential structures, such as new homes,

When undergoing training to become a plumber, students learn many techniques required for the job. This student is learning how to drill holes in concrete.

apartment high-rises, or college dorms. They also might work on commercial structures, such as baseball stadiums, shopping malls, or restaurants. Each kind of new building requires its own specific plumbing system. Some kinds of buildings, such as fire stations, scientific laboratories, and hospitals, might have special plumbing needs.

Plumbers are also called upon to install fixtures like bathtubs, showers, and toilets. Fixtures are devices that are attached to a wall or floor. Plumbing fixtures use water and usually have a pipe bringing water in and a drain to let water out. Plumbers also install appliances that use water, but are not necessarily attached to the wall or floor, such as dishwashers, hot water heaters, and washing machines.

In addition to putting in fixtures and appliances, plumbers install gas lines for stoves and heating systems. They install all the pipes that bring the water to kitchen and bath fixtures, as well as the pipes that take water away from them to sewer lines or septic tanks. Plumbers also fix and maintain the pipes and fixtures they install. They may also work on remodeling projects in kitchens or bathrooms. Or, they might update the plumbing in an existing home to accommodate the homeowner's needs. For instance, if a couple decides that they want to heat their home with natural gas, they will hire a plumber to run a new gas line into the home.

A plumber may specialize in a particular type of work. However, most plumbers know how to do many types of jobs. They might do several different types of job over the course of a week or even during a single workday.

WORKING CONDITIONS

Most plumbers work a regular workweek. That means they work Monday through Friday, from about 9:00 AM to

5:00 PM. However, some plumbers work for twenty-four-hour repair services. These plumbers are "on call." This means they must be available to fix an emergency, such as a burst pipe.

In the past, large buildings, power plants, and manufacturing plants often had full-time plumbers on staff. Now it is more common for such places to rely on outside companies for their plumbing needs. Therefore, more plumbers today work for twenty-four-hour repair services than in the past.

A plumber's workload is usually steady, although he or she may be busier at certain times of the year than others. New construction generally occurs in the spring through fall in most parts of the country, so there is usually more work available for plumbers during this time. Plumbers may work on indoor remodeling projects during the winter and might also be called upon to perform repair work on heating systems or to mend burst pipes.

TRYING OUT THE JOB

A good way for someone to decide if he or she would like to be a plumber is to work as a plumber's helper. Plumbers sometimes hire high school students or young adults for summer or year-round work. The helper assists the plumber in many different tasks. Although the work can be tiring and difficult, it is a great way to learn what a plumber does. Plumber's helpers see all of the day-to-day tasks plumbers perform. To find work as a plumber's helper, students can contact a plumber's union in their area. School guidance counselors or local job boards may also be good resources for help finding plumber's helper job openings.

Sometimes a plumber will work on a big, temporary project. For example, a plumber might work on the construction of a new hospital. When the project is done, the plumber might be out of work until his or her next project starts. Most

This plumber is volunteering his time to install a gas pipe in a Habitat for Humanity home in California. Habitat for Humanity is an organization that constructs housing for people in need.

of the time, however, successful plumbers go right from one project to the next.

Being a plumber can be a dirty job. When doing indoor work, plumbers often have to operate in dusty or dirty buildings or in small, cramped spaces. Outdoors, plumbers must often work in difficult weather conditions. They must be careful to observe the proper safety practices while at the work site, as many work sites can be dangerous if workers are not careful. To avoid injury, plumbers need to be aware of the danger posed by saws and sharp pipes. They must also be careful to avoid getting burned while using welding torches or working on steam pipes, and to avoid falls when working on ladders or scaffolding.

chapter 2

RELATED CAREERS

As mentioned earlier, some plumbers pursue a related career as a pipe fitter, pipe layer, steamfitter, or sprinkler fitter. These four careers have qualifications and career paths that are similar to general plumbing. Pipe fitters and pipe layers often work closely with plumbers.

PIPE FITTERS

Pipe fitters install and fix systems of pipes in buildings. They may install pipes that are part of a building's heating system. Or, they might work on pipe systems that are part of a plant that manufactures chemicals, drugs, or other products. Pipe fitters also set up the controls that monitor pipe systems. These control systems can start or stop the flow of liquids or steam through the pipes, and can turn on the timers and other mechanisms that start or stop the flow of fluids or gas automatically.

Like some plumbers, pipe fitters may work full time in one particular building. In general, however, pipe fitters are employed by companies that build or maintain pipe systems. In this capacity, pipe fitters might need to travel as part of their job. Pipe fitters might also work for a town

Pipe fitters use specialized tools to cut pipes. Different kinds of pipes require different kinds of cutting tools.

or city water department. Because they often work on multistory buildings that are still under construction, pipe fitters must not be afraid of heights. Some pipe fitters specialize in using one type of pipe material or one type of pipe system. For example, a pipe fitter might specialize in working with pipes that carry chemicals. Others work on all kinds of pipes and pipe systems.

PIPE LAYERS

Pipe layers prepare the area where pipes will go. A pipe layer may dig a trench for a pipe by hand, using a shovel, or by using a backhoe or other digging equipment. Once the trench is dug, pipe layers position the pipe in the trench. When the pipe is in position, the pipe layer attaches the pieces of pipe together. Depending on the pipe material, they may use cement or glue, or pipe layers may weld it together.

Pipe layers most often work outside. Sometimes they work

This plumber is installing a pipe in a trench prepared by a pipe layer. Pipe layers and plumbers often work together on new construction projects.

THE TRANS-ALASKA PIPELINE SYSTEM

Sometimes pipe layers work under very challenging conditions. The pipe layers who worked on the Trans-Alaska Pipeline System had to lay 800 miles (1,288 km) of pipes through frozen ground and mountain ranges. The pipeline also had to cross more than eight hundred rivers and streams. The Trans-Alaska Pipeline System is one of the longest in the world. It carries oil from northern areas of Alaska to the port of Valdez, Alaska. It took about twenty thousand workers more than two years to complete the pipeline.

in remote areas or under difficult weather conditions. Like pipe fitters, they might work for a company that builds or maintains pipe systems in various locations. Other pipe layers might work for an employer in one location. For example, they might work for a city or town public works department. They could be called upon to lay pipes for a municipal water system, or for other public utilities.

STEAMFITTERS

The duties of a steamfitter are similar to those of a pipe fitter. Steamfitters put in pipe systems just as pipe fitters do. The difference is that the pipes that steamfitters install are used to move water or gas that is under pressure. For that reason, steamfitters need additional training to know how to handle hot liquids and gases. Steamfitters must be certified to do this type of work as well. Like pipe fitters, steamfitters sometimes work on tall buildings that are under construction. Steamfitters usually

These workers oversee the construction of a section of the Trans-Alaska Pipeline System. Special supports allowed portions of the Trans-Alaska Pipeline System to be installed above the ground.

work for companies that install steam pipe systems in many different buildings, rather than working for an employer in a single building. They may also be on call to fix emergencies on nights or weekends.

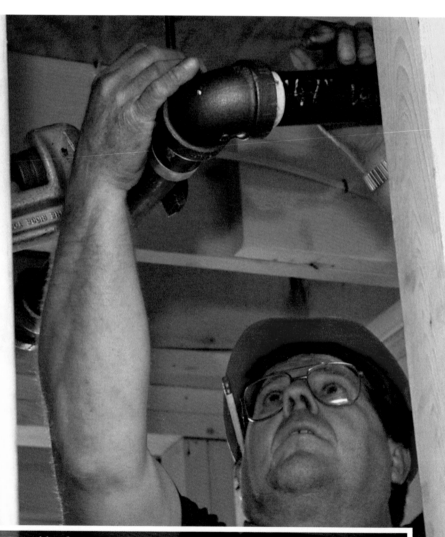

Sprinkler fitters install the pipes that carry water or other fire retardants. The sprinkler heads spray the water or fire retardant around the room.

SPRINKLER FITTERS

Sprinkler fitters install fire protection systems and fix existing systems. Fire protection systems include sprinklers, pipes, and

hoses. Some systems use water to put out fires, while others use chemical fire retardants such as foam.

Sprinkler systems are usually not installed in houses or small apartment buildings. Instead they are installed in public buildings like offices, schools, high-rise apartment buildings, restaurants, or manufacturing plants. Some states and cities are considering requiring sprinkler systems in additional types of buildings, including residential buildings. As a result, sprinkler fitters may have even more work in the coming years.

chapter 3

PREPARING
TO BE A PLUMBER

There are several different paths to becoming a plumber. Students who already know they would like to become a plumber have several options. After high school, they can go straight to work as an apprentice plumber. Or, they can go to college or attend a trade school before becoming an apprentice plumber. Some people work in another career before deciding to become a plumber. For instance, they might work for several years as a pipe fitter before deciding to become a plumber. Some people become plumbers after spending time in a completely unrelated career as well.

It's never too soon for junior high and high school students to begin preparing themselves for a career in plumbing. Professional plumbers need to have good math skills to do their job. Taking math classes, especially algebra and geometry, can be an especially good way to prepare for this career. Because plumbers often work with a variety of materials, science classes like physics and chemistry are also useful. Alongside these academic courses, it is a good idea to take classes in drafting and mechanical drawing. Technical education classes can teach students how to properly use a variety of tools, as well as the fundamentals of skills such as welding.

VOCATIONAL SCHOOLS

Students who are interested in pursuing a career in plumbing may choose to go to vocational school, rather than the last year or two of high school. Vocational schools (which are also sometimes called trade schools) provide students with the skills and training needed for a particular career, such as car repair, carpentry, and plumbing.

However, they also offer students many of the same kinds of classes they would take in high school, such as English or history. Students interested in attending a vocational school should talk to their school guidance counselor for more information. If there is a vocational school nearby, students can also arrange a visit to learn more.

TECHNICAL SCHOOL AND COMMUNITY COLLEGE

After graduating from vocational school or high school, people who want to become plumbers can attend community college or a technical school. Technical schools are similar to vocational schools. They also teach particular skills that will help prepare a student for a future career. Technical school programs are usually two years long. Some community colleges offer skill-specific classes as well. At most community colleges, you can get an associate's degree after two years or a bachelor's degree after four years.

At community college or technical school, students can learn how to read plumbing blueprints. They will also begin learning about specific plumbing codes. In addition, students will learn special skills, such as welding. Perhaps most importantly, students can take safety classes so that they know how to stay safe on the job.

These two students are learning to bend a conduit at a trade school sponsored by a power company.

MAKING THE RIGHT CHOICE

After graduating from high school or vocational school, students interested in becoming plumbers have a decision to make. They can continue their education, or they can go straight to work. Although recommended, attending a vocational school, technical school, or community college is not a requirement for becoming a plumber. Some plumbers leave high school and immediately start working. Beginning plumbers do an apprenticeship and take classes at night or on weekends. Every person is different, so there is no one right way. A student's choice may depend on his or her personality, financial situation, or goals. There are benefits and drawbacks to each choice. When making the decision, students should carefully weigh their options.

An advantage of continuing to community college or technical school is that students can learn from experts. Teachers are available to answer questions. Students are also part of a community and can discuss what they're learning with their classmates. By working together, students at a community college can have a richer learning experience than they might have had trying to figure things out by themselves. Another advantage of school is that students can take classes in specialized topics relevant to plumbing. These classes give students a head start when they begin an apprenticeship program.

A disadvantage of community college or technical school is that it costs money. Students will most likely not be able to work a full-time job while attending college and will have to work around their class schedule. However, many schools offer scholarships, grants, and other forms of financial aid that can help defray the cost of tuition.

Some high school or vocational school graduates decide to begin an apprenticeship program. There are advantages and

One of the advantages of attending community college is that students can take classes in subjects such as communication or business.

disadvantages to going straight to work in an apprenticeship program. One advantage is that apprentices earn a regular salary. More important, they also get hands-on experience working with professional plumbers. Apprentices can also create their own study schedule on nights or weekends.

A disadvantage to entering an apprenticeship program right after high school is that students don't get to learn from teachers and don't get the experience of interacting with other students. People who go straight to work also miss out on other, non-plumbing classes they could take at a community college. For example, students interested in owning their own plumbing business some day can take accounting and business management classes while at community college.

Students who want more help with the decision of whether to apply to school or begin working should speak with their school guidance counselor. A guidance counselor can not only provide

Plumbing Codes

Building codes are regulations set up by state and local governments. They are written to make sure that buildings are safe for the people who live and work in them. Some building codes are specific to plumbing. These rules and regulations are created so that people have safe drinking water, for example. The codes are also designed to do things like prevent accidents or explosions. Plumbing codes specify safety measures for any plumbing work done in a factory, home, hospital, office, or school. A large part of a plumber's education is learning and understanding all plumbing codes.

students with valuable career advice, but can also help them find information about community colleges, trade schools, and apprenticeship programs.

Job Corps

The U.S. Department of Labor runs a program called Job Corps for teens and young adults. The Job Corps offers courses in several construction trades, including plumbing. The program also helps teens and young adults ages sixteen to twenty-four earn their high school diploma or General Educational Development (GED) diploma. Once students have completed the program, Job Corps helps them create résumés and find employment. An excellent option for those who are having a difficult time affording college, this program is free to anyone who qualifies for it.

Military Training

Aspiring plumbers who don't want to go straight to work and don't want to attend community college or a trade school have another option: They can join the military. Joining the military is an additional way to prepare for a career in plumbing or pipe fitting. Plumbers and pipe fitters are needed in every branch of the military. Enlistees receive training in plumbing and pipe fitting in return for their service. This training is very similar to the kind of training that they would receive in class or in an apprenticeship outside of the military.

Military plumbers and pipe fitters install and maintain pipe systems in buildings, ships, and aircraft. The experience that people gain from plumbing and pipe fitting in the military can be a great help when they attempt to establish a civilian plumbing career. Military plumbing experience can reduce the number of hours they have to spend in the classroom, or as an apprentice, before becoming a licensed plumber.

chapter 4

APPRENTICESHIP PROGRAMS

D uring an apprenticeship program, the real work of being a plumber begins. An apprenticeship consists of getting actual, hands-on experience by working alongside an experienced plumber, known as a master plumber. During this time, apprentices learn everything they will need to know to become a licensed plumber.

WHAT IS AN APPRENTICESHIP PROGRAM?

Apprenticeships are on-the-job training programs. In addition to working with experienced plumbers, apprentices also take classes at night or on weekends. In some apprenticeship programs, apprentices work four days a week and attend classes one day a week. Most apprenticeship programs last four or five years. Each year, apprentices are expected to spend about two thousand hours working and about one hundred and fifty to two hundred hours taking classes. Apprenticeship programs vary from state to state and from program to program.

Working with a master plumber, apprentices learn to read blueprints and building plans so that they will know where to place pipes. They become familiar with the varieties of pipes and other plumbing materials, study building codes and

Apprentices work with experienced plumbers to learn all aspects of plumbing. This apprentice is learning to solder by watching a master plumber.

become familiar with important safety procedures, and learn how to use all the tools needed to get the job done.

REQUIREMENTS FOR APPRENTICESHIP PROGRAMS

Apprentices must be at least eighteen years old and in good physical condition. In many cases, apprentices must have graduated from high school or have a GED. Apprenticeship programs often require that apprentices have a driver's license, and many programs require that apprentices pass a drug test. A birth certificate, or another document that proves that applicants are eighteen or older, as well as documentation proving that the applicant is a citizen or legal immigrant, is sometimes requested.

All plumbers' work must meet the requirements of building inspectors, which means that apprentice plumbers must familiarize themselves with local building codes.

Apprenticeships are generally run by unions or contractor organizations. Here is a list of organizations that sponsor plumbing apprenticeships:

- American Fire Sprinkler Association
- Associated Builders and Contractors

COURSES REQUIRED

In addition to the on-the-job training, apprentices spend time in the classroom. There they learn more about math, science, safety, first aid, many types of plumber's tools, various pipe systems, and many other topics. They also learn how to weld, how to work with natural gas, and how to read blueprints and plans. The course requirements for a plumber's apprentice can vary by state. Here is an overview of courses required in the state of Massachusetts:

- Practical arithmetic
- Basic algebra
- Plane geometry
- Trigonometry
- Blueprint reading
- Elementary architectural drawing
- Drawing and sketching
- Specification writing
- Types of pipes and fittings
- Hot water heating piping systems
- Sewage systems
- Plumbing and pipe fitting tools
- Pipe fitting practice
- Welding practice
- Clay, iron, and vent systems
- Occupational Safety and Health Act (OSHA)
- Sanitary plumbing fixtures
- Installation of gas appliances and piping

- Home Builders Institute of the National Association of Home Builders
- Mechanical Contractors Association of America
- Plumbing-Heating-Cooling Contractors Association
- National Fire Sprinkler Association
- United Association of Journeymen and Apprentices of the Plumbing and Pipe Fitting Industry of the United States and Canada

To find a local apprenticeship, students can check with one of these organizations or with their state's employment and training office.

This teacher prepares her students to take the GED. To participate in most apprenticeship programs, applicants must have a high school diploma or GED.

WAGES AND BENEFITS

Apprentice plumbers usually make about half the salary of what experienced plumbers earn. As apprentices gain more experience, their wages go up. The kind of benefits they receive, such as health insurance, depend on the union they belong to or their employer. Apprentices usually receive benefits such as health insurance, as well as pensions and retirement savings plans.

TIPS FOR SUCCEEDING IN AN APPRENTICESHIP

The Plumbers Union Local 5 in Washington, D.C., offers these general tips for succeeding as an apprentice on their Web site:

1. Pay attention to what the master plumber has to say. Don't talk too much or offer an opinion unless the plumber asks for an opinion.

2. Show interest in learning all aspects of the job.

3. Help the plumber in whatever tasks he or she requests. An apprentice's job is to learn, but also to assist the plumber.

4. Respect the plumber's way of working, and respect the importance of the job.

5. Work hard. The harder an apprentice works, the harder the master plumber will work to teach him or her.

Other Things Learned During an Apprenticeship

Apprentices learn more than just plumbing skills from the plumbers who train them. For example, if they work in residential plumbing, apprentices will learn good communication skills and how to work well with customers. Plumbers who own their own business might also teach apprentices how to run their own company some day. If apprentices work in commercial plumbing, they'll learn to work on a team with other contractors. For example, commercial plumbers might need to interact with electricians, elevator installers, and heating or air-conditioning technicians.

chapter 5

WORKING AS A PLUMBER

Plumbers perform many jobs. The two main tasks of plumbers are installation and repair. Plumbers install new pipes and pipe systems. On residential jobs, plumbers may install plumbing and appliances. When plumbers work on commercial jobs, they may also install specialized equipment. For example, a plumber might install a special pipe system in a laboratory that uses hazardous chemicals.

The other main task plumbers perform is repair. They find and fix leaks in pipes, faucets, and water lines. They unclog pipes and drains. During the winter, plumbers may also repair damaged pipes. Cold temperatures can cause the water inside pipes to freeze, and therefore expand, busting the pipe. Over time, some types of pipe can also crack, causing serious leaks.

Sometimes plumbers are called upon to "rescue" things that have accidentally gone down a drain, such as expensive rings or other jewelry. In some cases, plumbers use a cable with a small camera attached to locate the object. When the plumber finds the item, he or she can sometimes grab it with small pincers and pull it out. Other times, the fixture must be taken off the floor or wall in order to locate the missing object.

AN EXAMPLE OF A JOB FROM START TO FINISH

When starting a residential job on a house under construction, the first thing a plumber would do is look over the blueprints and building plans from the architect and contractor. The plans tell the plumber where the fixtures will go. The plumber makes note of where the water line will come in from the street. He or she will also note where the sewage line, which connects the house to the municipal sewage system or a septic tank, will go.

Based on the plans, the plumber will begin to lay out where the pipes will need to be placed. Once the pipes are roughly laid out, the plumber marks on the walls, ceilings, or floors where the pipes will go. He or she notes obstacles the pipes will need to go around, such as lines for electricity. The plumber then takes careful measurements so that he or she will have pipes of the correct length. The plumber must also make sure that installing pipes will not cause any other problems with the building. For instance, if the pipes are too heavy, they could pull away from their support and damage a wall or ceiling. Some

appliances, such as washing machines, bathtubs or showers, need several pipes. These fixtures need separate pipes for hot and cold water and a pipe to drain away wastewater. The plumber will also need to make sure that the plumbing in the house conforms to local building codes.

This plumber has been hired to fix a clogged kitchen sink. He used an auger fed down a plumbing vent on the roof to unclog the drain.

When all marking and measuring is complete, the plumber begins cutting holes in walls, floors, or ceilings. The holes will allow the pipes to be attached to fixtures. After holes have been cut for every pipe, the plumber begins putting the pipes in

Part of a plumber's job is being able to read and understand blueprints. Blueprints allow plumbers to understand how a building's plumbing layout will work.

place. Sometimes pipes must be hung using metal supports, and other times they are laid underground.

With the straight pipes in place, the plumber begins hooking them together with connectors. Connectors can be U-shaped, or they can be bent at an angle. This type of connector can connect a horizontal pipe to a vertical pipe. If a plumber is using metal pipes, sometimes he or she can bend them into the correct angle. Once the pipes are correctly connected, the plumber can begin to securely attach the pipes to each other. Pipes are attached using a number of different methods.

The next step is to attach the fixtures to the pipes. How the fixtures are attached depends on the fixture and the type of pipe being used. When all the pipes are attached to fixtures, the plumber begins testing all parts of the system. He or she turns all faucets on and off to make sure water is flowing and draining correctly. The plumber also checks the water pressure to make sure water is getting through pipes at the correct rate. If water is flowing too slowly or too quickly, the plumber must make adjustments.

Finally, a plumber must also set up a system of traps and vents. Traps are attached to the pipe that drains water away from a fixture, such as a sink. The trap holds a little of the water inside, which prevents gas from the sewer from coming up into the house or building. Vents go outside the building—usually through a roof—to allow air into the plumbing system. The air helps keep water flowing correctly.

A new residential construction job can last from several days to a week or more. The length of the job depends on the size of the house, how many fixtures must be installed, and how many bathrooms are in the house. The time needed can increase if the plumber discovers any problems in the construction, or if he or she runs into difficulties with municipal water, gas, or sewer pipes.

Plumbers must have a good set of tools for installation and repair. This plumber uses a wrench to tighten a leaky pipe under a sink, which is connected to the sink's trap.

TOOLS OF THE TRADE

A plumber relies on many types of tools to get the job done. The types of tools used vary depending on the project, but most plumbers will have a wide variety of basic tools on hand. Sometimes plumbers will need to transport tools, pipes, and other supplies to the job site, so most of them own a truck or a van.

MEASURING TOOLS

Before plumbers begin a job, they spend time carefully measuring where pipes will go. Plumbers sometimes use a regular tape measure. For jobs that must be extremely accurate, they generally use a steel rule (a rigid and accurate ruler). Plumbers often mark their measurements with an ordinary pencil or pen, although they might also use a permanent marker to make darker lines that won't wear off. To make markings on sheet metal or metal pipes, plumbers can use a tool called a scriber. Plumbers use a tool called a center punch to mark the exact center of a circle where a hole will be drilled.

DEMOLITION AND CUTTING TOOLS

For remodeling projects and repairs, plumbers may need to get rid of existing pipes, floors, walls, or ceilings. They might also need to dig out old pipe with a chisel or use pry bars to pull out old or damaged floors or walls.

In the course of a workday, plumbers also use many different types of cutting tools. Tin snips can be used to cut sheet metal. Some types of tin snips can cut curves, while others are better at cutting straight lines. Plumbers often use tubing cutters to cut pipes, although some kinds of pipe require special tools to cut. Copper pipe is generally cut with hacksaws, and chain-link cutters can be used to cut wide cast-iron pipe. The links on chain-link cutters look like a bicycle chain. They can be wrapped around pipes of various sizes. The links are then tightened to cut through the pipe. Plumbers carry wire cutters, as well as a few different types of files. Files are used to smooth the rough edges that are left after metal is cut.

WRENCHES

Plumbers always have many wrenches with them on a job. Wrenches are used to loosen or tighten fasteners, and they also help plumbers get a good grip on a pipe. There are many types of wrenches, including adjustable, basin, pipe, socket, and strap wrenches. Plumbers usually have many wrenches in a variety of sizes.

SOLDERING IRONS AND TORCHES

Plumbers use specialized tools to connect pipe together. One such tool is a soldering iron. Solder is a mixture of metals that melt at a lower temperature than the pipe the plumber wants to join together. Solder comes in wire form or as a bar.

Plumbers use a tool called a soldering iron to heat the solder until it melts. The plumber then applies the melted solder to both halves of a pipe. When the solder cools, it also hardens, and the pipes are securely connected. When using thicker pipes, plumbers use a different tool to melt the solder. This is called a heat torch, which is powered by propane and other types of gases. A heat torch can create much higher temperatures, which are better for melting solder.

This plumber is using a welding torch and a spool of soldering wire to seal the connection on a pipe.

PLUNGERS AND AUGERS

To clear blocked pipes and drains, plumbers use plungers and augers. Plungers clear blockages by sucking air and water out of the drain and then forcing it back in. (Many households have plungers on hand to clear simple blockages.) Augers are flexible tubes with special attachments on the end. A plumber feeds an auger into a blocked pipe. When it reaches the blockage, the plumber twists the attachments to loosen the blockage. Sometimes plumbers attach augers to an electric drill. The drill helps rotate the attachments to exert more force on the blockage.

GENERAL AND SAFETY TOOLS

Plumbers carry many common tools that anyone might have for use in his or her home, such as pocketknives, hammers, and screwdrivers. They always have a flashlight or two on hand to see into dark spaces. Plumbers also use mirrors to see around corners when working on a job where space is limited. On the job, plumbers generally just wear jeans or other long pants and a T-shirt. Since plumbing can be a dirty job, some plumbers wear coveralls to keep their regular clothing clean.

Safety is an important concern for plumbers, and they usually wear eye protection when using cutting tools. They also generally use protective gear, especially protective goggles, when using welding torches. Plumbers protect their hands with gloves when working with sharp metal or hot materials. To protect their feet from falling pipes or tools, they generally wear steel-toed boots. Large construction sites often require all workers, including plumbers, to wear hard hats for their protection.

Plastic pipes are often held together with powerful glue. This plumber is using a protective mask while working with the glue to protect him from fumes.

TYPES OF PIPE

When putting in new pipes in homes, plumbers most often use ones made of copper, plastic, or steel. Residential projects

Pipes made out of PVC are extremely durable and are often found in private residences. Plumbers can purchase PVC pipes and other supplies from home improvement stores or plumbing supply companies.

usually don't require a lot of water to flow through pipes. So smaller pipes are generally used for these projects. One or two plumbers or plumber's helpers can install these kinds of pipes.

Plastic pipes are commonly used in residences. There are several types of plastic pipe, including PVC, CPVC, PEX, and PolyPipe. Some of these pipes are used for specialized purposes. For example, PVC is only used for cold water. PolyPipe is often used to connect a house's plumbing system to a city or town water supply, as it is harder than other types of plastic pipe and can carry more water.

Copper pipe is also used in homes. It can carry hot or cold water. In some older homes, galvanized steel was used. If plumbers make repairs to older homes, they must know how to work with galvanized pipe. Today, many plumbers will simply update plumbing systems by replacing galvanized pipe with newer types of pipes. Plumbers also use small tubes for some small jobs. For example, tubing is used to connect an automatic ice maker in a refrigerator to a water supply.

Larger pipes facilitate the movement of larger volumes of

FIRST AID

Although plumbing is not necessarily a dangerous job, injuries can occur. It can be a good idea for plumbers to take first-aid classes. They should know how to treat common injuries, such as minor cuts and blisters, as well as more serious injuries. People who have serious injuries sometimes go into shock, and it's useful for plumbers to be able to recognize the symptoms of shock. This way, they can help people who are in shock until paramedics arrive. Because plumbers occasionally work outside during the hot summer months, they should also know how to identify and treat heatstroke. Most apprentices take safety and first-aid classes as part of their training.

water. For instance, the pipes that are used in sewers, or in municipal water supply systems, need to be very large to cope with the amount of fluid that flows through them. These pipes are generally made from cast iron. To install large pipes such as these, plumbers need to work with a team. The team might include experienced pipe layers and pipe fitters. Together, they use machinery to dig trenches for the pipes and to move them. This is specialized work that plumbers need to be trained in.

ATTACHING PIPES

Plumbers use a number of methods to join pipes. Different materials are used to connect different types of pipe. For instance, a plumber can use screws or bolts to connect metal pipes. Metal pipes can also be soldered together. Plastic pipes can be joined by specialized glue.

Many pipes are joined with small devices called fittings. One type of fitting is called a coupling. A coupling is a short length of pipe, usually of the same material as the pipes being attached. Couplings can attach pipes of the same size or pipes that are two different sizes. Other fittings connect more than two pipes. Tees attach three pipes together. They are called tees because they look like the letter "T." They connect two pipes in a straight line and a third pipe perpendicular to the other two. Plumbers use a fitting called a cross to connect four pipes.

Plumbers also use fittings to create a bend in a pipe. These fittings are called elbows, or "ells." Like couplings, they can connect pipes of the same size or of two different sizes. Fittings such as caps and plugs can be put on one end of a pipe to seal it off.

chapter 6

GETTING A LICENSE AND BEGINNING A CAREER

Getting a license is an important step for a plumber's career. Licensed plumbers not only make a higher salary, but they also supervise unlicensed plumbers on a job site. Plumbers can take their licensing exam once they've finished their apprenticeship.

GETTING A PLUMBING LICENSE

Licensing exams vary from one place to another. To get a license, a plumber must pass a test on a variety of plumbing skills, as well as the local plumbing codes. In most places, there are two different tests: one for a journeyperson and one for a master plumber. Journeyperson licenses are for people who have finished their apprenticeships and have worked as a plumber for a

certain number of years. Master licenses are for plumbers who already have a journeyperson license and have also worked for a required number of hours and taken additional night or weekend classes.

In addition to licenses for journeypersons and master plumbers, some states also have an additional license called a residential license. This license is for plumbers who have finished an apprenticeship, but have not worked for as many years as a journeyperson.

Some apprentices choose to take test preparation classes in order to prepare for licensing exams. This student, who wants to become a professional plumber, is receiving help from a tutor.

It isn't possible for a plumber to get certified nationally. Instead, each state or local town has different licensing requirements and exams. Plumbers must be familiar with their state and local plumbing codes. If a plumber moves to a

Radiant heating is composed of a system of tubes that carry hot water. These are installed underneath the floor of a residence.

different state or city, he or she must get a new license to work in the area.

Licensing exams are usually made up of multiple choice, true or false, and fill-in-the-blank questions. These tests have questions on topics such as:

- Local plumbing codes
- Typical plumbing fixtures used in homes
- Specialized fixtures, such as large dishwashers used in restaurants
- The procedure for connecting a building to a public sewage system
- Types of pipe to use for particular jobs

Licensing exams can be difficult, and it is not unusual for someone to fail the test the first time. However, anyone who studies hard can eventually pass the test. Libraries and bookstores carry test preparation books that can help plumbers pass the exam. In addition, many colleges and trade schools offer test preparation classes that can also help. These classes are usually held on nights and weekends. However, taking a class isn't always necessary— plumbers can also study on their

AN INTERVIEW WITH A PLUMBER

Casey Connell is a licensed plumber from Walpole, Massachusetts. He held several other jobs until settling on a rewarding career in plumbing.

What do you like about plumbing?
I like to be able to work with my hands and to work on a project from start to finish. I also like being able to work independently. Plumbing is a good trade. There are good opportunities for working your way up. For example, you can become an estimator or project manager. You can also start your own business.

What was your career path?
I worked in a few different fields before becoming a plumber. I worked in landscaping and did some concrete work. Then I began fixing and installing oil burners. When I was thirty years old, I began working as a plumber's apprentice and went to night school. I served three years of an apprenticeship and then took the licensing exam. (My state now requires a five-year apprenticeship, but at the time I did it, my apprenticeship was only three years long.)

What do you recommend students do if they want to be a plumber?
I would recommend going to vocational school. You should definitely study math. Geometry can help you a lot.

What should people do to prepare for the licensing exam?
You don't necessarily need to take an exam preparation class. Most people do OK studying on their own for the exam. However, you have to put time into studying if you want to pass.

Do you see good opportunities for people who want to be plumbers?
Yes, there is going to be a huge demand in the coming years. Many plumbers will be retiring soon. And, although the building boom is over, a lot of existing buildings are being retrofitted with green improvements.

own for the exam. Public libraries sometimes have online practice tests or classes that plumbers can take. Some plumbers choose to study with another plumber who is also preparing to take the licensing exam, or get help from plumbers who have already passed the exam.

OPPORTUNITIES IN GREEN PLUMBING

In the coming years, many houses and buildings will be "going green." Making environmentally friendly improvements in a building's plumbing can save homeowners or business owners money in water or energy costs. And, of course, it also helps the environment by preserving natural resources.

Green plumbers can play a big role in making buildings more energy efficient and environmentally friendly, and there are several types of green changes that plumbers can make in homes and buildings. An example of a simple change is installing high-efficiency fixtures, such as toilets, low-flow showers, and environmentally friendly washing machines. These fixtures and appliances use much less water than older models. For people who are even more serious about greening their building, plumbers can make more extensive changes as well. For instance, they might install radiant heating or solar heating systems, or they may design and install gray water systems.

Plumbers can take courses in green plumbing to add to their set of skills. Trade and vocational schools are adding

Many homes are now utilizing green technologies to save on energy bills. Here, a worker checks an environmentally friendly heating system in a housing complex.

courses in green technology to their plumbing training programs. Some schools and companies also offer courses for certifying plumbers in green technologies.

HIGH-EFFICIENCY FIXTURES

There have been many advances in green plumbing fixtures. More and more fixtures are being designed to use less water. For example, some newer toilets use much less water than older toilets. These are called low-flow or high-efficiency toilets. Other toilets compost waste, rather than using any water to flush. Some modern urinals actually use no water at all. Front-loading washing machines use much less water than top-loading machines, and modern dishwashers use less water than older models.

HEATING SYSTEMS

Two types of green heating systems rely on plumbing to operate. These are solar heating systems and radiant heating systems. Solar systems use solar energy to generate electricity and to warm water or create electricity. Radiant heat consists of small pipes or tubes that are concealed underneath flooring and carry hot water. This heat radiates upward from the floor. Since radiant heating is so efficient, it costs homeowners less money to heat their building. Sometimes radiant heating is installed in the walls or ceilings of a building as well.

At one time, plumbing was considered to be a job that was only done by men. In recent years, however, more women have been entering the plumbing profession.

GRAY WATER SYSTEMS

Gray water recycling systems are another popular green plumbing technology. Gray water is wastewater generated by dishwashers, washing machines, sinks, and showers. Gray water can be stored and then reused to water outdoor plants. Sometimes gray water is filtered or processed. It can then be used as water to be flushed in toilets, for example. Plumbers can create and install gray water systems in homes and other buildings.

WOMEN IN PLUMBING

In 2008, there were approximately 8,000 female plumbers working in the United States, as well as 484,000 male plumbers. Traditionally, plumbing has been considered a "male only" profession. Some people still believe that women can't handle the heavy physical work that male plumbers do. But this attitude is slowly changing, and many women are realizing that plumbing is a worthwhile career that pays well.

Women plumbers ultimately find that they can handle the

physical challenges of the job just as well as men. Susan McDaniel is a plumber who co-owns a plumbing business in North Carolina. In an article in *Plumbing and Mechanical* magazine, she explains that there are ways to approach the physical challenges of the job besides brute force. "I have to use my brain more when I have to lift things. My back isn't as strong, so I have to figure out alternative ways to move heavy items."

Currently, there are few role models for young female plumbers to look up to. Because of this, young women may not realize that there are opportunities in the plumbing profession. That may change as more women enter the profession. It can be helpful for young women who want to be plumbers to try and find a female plumber who works in their area. Experienced female plumbers may be willing to discuss the advantages of a career in plumbing or act as a mentor to a novice. Young women should also look for apprenticeship programs that specifically encourage women to apply.

Women have been a valuable part of the workforce for many decades now. However, the attitude of some male plumbers has not necessarily reflected that fact. In some cases, male plumbers have harassed their female colleagues. Many women profiled in an article in *Reeves Journal* about women in the plumbing industry say they have faced challenges from men in the profession. "I put up with insults and intimidation to prove I belonged in this industry," says plumber Tracy Belvill.

However, many female plumbers say that it is possible to get past those attitudes. Sometimes they even change sexist male plumber's minds by showing how well women can do the job. McDaniel offers the following advice for female plumbers: "Develop a thick skin, and [. . .] let your actions, ability and worth speak for you, rather than your anger."

This is not the only way in which female plumbers can face gender discrimination in the workplace, however. Sometimes, qualified female plumbers might not get hired for a job simply because they are not male. This is changing as cultural attitudes evolve. In addition, the need for competent plumbers is increasing. Some female plumbers avoid discrimination by starting their own business.

CAREER PATHS FOR LICENSED PLUMBERS

Once plumbers are licensed, they have several career options. Besides doing the same work as they did before, licensed plumbers can also train and supervise other plumbers. For example, a licensed master plumber can train an apprentice or journeyperson plumber. Licensed master plumbers can also become plumbing inspectors. Plumbing inspectors check the work of other plumbers to make sure it meets local plumbing codes.

Licensed plumbers can also become plumbing estimators. Estimators figure out how much time a project will take, what materials are needed, and how much the job will cost. They often work for companies that build large buildings or groups of buildings, such as apartment complexes. Estimators work with engineers and architects before a building project begins.

Plumbers that start their own business generally begin by working on their own or with a business partner. As their business builds, they can hire other people to work for them. In some cases, they might hire additional plumbers to help with the workload or other workers that can offer additional services. For instance, a business owner might hire a person to work on heating or air-conditioning systems or someone who can build or clean septic systems.

Plumbers can also apply their knowledge and expertise to other business pursuits. They might try their hand at starting their own plumbing supply company or starting a company that installs irrigation systems. These types of watering systems might

Some plumbers create family businesses and work with their relatives. This plumber bought his plumbing business from his father when he retired.

be used on farms to grow crops. Other types of irrigation systems might be set up on residential or business lawns or gardens.

THE FUTURE OF PLUMBING

No matter whether the economy is good or bad, there will always be opportunities for plumbers. Plumbers provide essential services. They keep showers and toilets working. They allow fresh water to flow into kitchens and laundry rooms. Plumbers repair broken hot water tanks and sewer lines. Every house, apartment building, school, supermarket, and factory will need a plumber at some time or another. Anyone who likes to make things work, and keep things working, should consider a career as a plumber.

glossary

blueprint A detailed building plan created by an architect.

citizen A legal resident of a country.

colleague An associate who works in the same profession.

commercial plumber A plumber who works on projects for businesses.

compost To break down organic matter in order to reuse it as a fertilizer.

conduit A pipe or tube that something can pass through.

consequence A result or effect.

contractor A person hired to get a particular job done.

coveralls A one-piece outfit worn over regular clothes.

defray To provide for the payment of something.

demolition The act of tearing down an existing structure.

disposable income Extra money that can be used to purchase items that are not necessities.

dormitory A building where many people can sleep, usually at a college.

fire retardant A substance that is used to put out or slow down a fire.

gender discrimination Treating people unfairly based on whether they are male or female.

legal immigrant Someone who has permission to live and work in a foreign country.

mechanism A piece of machinery.

municipal Something that is owned or operated by a city or town government.

obstacle Something that stands in the way of a goal or objective.

pension A salary paid to a worker after retirement.

perpendicular Forming a right angle with something else.

propane A gas that can be used as fuel.

qualification A special skill or knowledge.

remodel To change or improve a structure.

residential plumber A plumber who works on projects in private homes.

retrofit To install new parts or equipment in something that is older. For instance, a plumber might retrofit a home by replacing old fixtures with newer, more efficient ones.

salary Money paid to someone, generally at a regularly scheduled time, for work that he or she does.

scaffolding A temporary platform, or system of platforms, used to hold workers on a job site.

septic tank A tank in which sewage is broken down by bacteria.

sewage Waste material carried away by pipes.

for more information

Associated Builders and Contractors (ABC)
4250 N. Fairfax Drive, 9th Floor
Arlington, VA 22203-1607
(703) 812-2000
Web site: http://www.trytools.org
The ABC represents the interests of thousands of construction
firms in the United States. The association provides
numerous resources for students interested in joining the
plumbing and/or construction industry.

Canada Green Building Council (CaGBC)
47 Clarence Street, Suite 202
Ottawa, ON K1N 9K1
Canada
(866) 941-1184
Web site: http://www.cagbc.org
The CaGBC is a nonprofit organization dedicated to reduc-
ing the environmental impact of buildings.

GreenPlumbers
4153 Northgate Boulevard, Suite 1
Sacramento, CA 95834
(888) 929-6207
Web site: http://www.greenplumbersusa.com
GreenPlumbers offers training to plumbers interested in water
conservation practices and green plumbing products.

Home Builders Institute (HBI)
1201 15th Street NW, Sixth Floor
Washington, DC 20005-2800

(800) 959-0052
Web site: http://www.hbi.org
Part of the National Association of Home Builders (NAHB),
    the HBI helps train plumbers and many other profession-
    als in the construction industry.

Job Corps
U.S. Department of Labor
200 Constitution Avenue NW, Suite N4463
Washington, DC 20210
(800) 733-5627
Web site: http://www.jobcorps.gov
The Job Corps is a free job training and education program
    for people ages sixteen to twenty-four. Plumbing is one of
    the construction trades in the Job Corps program.

Mechanical Contractors Association of Canada
    (MCA Canada)
#601-280 Albert Street
Ottawa, ON K1P 5G8
Canada
(613) 232-0492
Web site: http://www.mcac.ca
MCA Canada is Canada's largest trade contractor's associa-
    tion. It works to promote, improve, and advance the
    mechanical contracting industry.

National Association of Women in Construction (NAWIC)
327 S. Adams Street
Fort Worth, TX 76104
(800) 552-3506
Web site: http://www.nawic.org
The NAWIC is an association made up of women working in
    the construction industry.

National Center for Construction Education
    and Research (NCCER)
3600 NW 43rd Street, Building G
Gainesville, FL 32606
(888) 622-3720
Web site: http://www.nccer.org
The NCCER is a nonprofit foundation whose goal is to
    standardize training for workers in the construction
    industry.

Plumbing-Heating-Cooling Contractors Association (PHCC)
180 S. Washington Street
P.O. Box 6808
Falls Church, VA 22046
(800) 533-7694
Web site: http://phccweb.org
The oldest trade association in the construction industry, the
    PHCC promotes education and training.

United Association of Journeymen and Apprentices in the
    Plumbing and Pipe Fitting Industry of the United States
    and Canada (UA)
United Association Building
Three Park Place
Annapolis, MD 21401
(410) 269-2000
Web site: http://www.ua.org
The UA is a union that represents more than three hundred
    thousand plumbers and pipe fitters in the United States
    and Canada.

U.S. Department of Labor
Employment and Training Administration (ETA)
Frances Perkins Building

200 Constitution Avenue NW
Washington, DC 20210
(877) 872-5627
Web site: http://www.doleta.gov
The ETA offers information on apprenticeship programs and
   other training options for aspiring plumbers.

U.S. Green Building Council (USGBC)
2101 L Street NW, Suite 500
Washington, DC 20037
Web site: http://www.usgbc.org
The USGBC is a nonprofit organization dedicated to green
   building and construction. It has a program called
   Emerging Green Builders (EGB) that students and
   young professionals can join to get involved in local
   green building projects.

Web Sites

Due to the changing nature of Internet links, Rosen Publishing
has developed an online list of Web sites related to the subject
of this book. This site is updated regularly. Please use this link
to access the list:

http://www.rosenlinks.com/ecar/plum

for further reading

Cassio, Jim, and Alice Rush. *Green Careers: Choosing Work for a Sustainable Future.* Gabriola Island, BC: New Society Publishers, 2009.

Eberts, Marjorie. *Careers for Hard Hats and Other Construction Types.* New York, NY: McGraw-Hill, 2009.

Frew, Katherine. *Plumber.* New York, NY: Rosen Publishing Group, Inc., 2004.

JIST Editors. *Young Person's Occupational Outlook Handbook.* 6th ed. Indianapolis, IN: JIST Works, 2007.

Lamacchia, Joe, and Bridget Samburg. *Blue Collar and Proud of It: The All-in-One Resource for Finding Freedom, Financial Success, and Security Outside the Cubicle.* Deerfield Beach, FL: Health Communications, Inc., 2009.

McGraw-Hill Editors and the U.S. Department of Labor, Bureau of Labor Statistics. *The Big Book of Jobs.* 2007– 2008 ed. New York, NY: McGraw-Hill, 2007.

Mondschein, Kenneth C. *Great Careers with a High School Diploma: Construction and Trades.* New York, NY: Ferguson Publishing, 2008.

National Center for Construction Education and Research. *Careers in Construction.* Upper Saddle River, NJ: Prentice Hall, 2007.

Rich, Jason. *202 High-Paying Jobs You Can Land Without a College Degree.* Irvine, CA: Entrepreneur Press, 2006.

Sumichrast, Michael, and David Davitaia. *Opportunities in Building Construction Careers.* New York, NY: McGraw-Hill, 2008.

Weiss, Jodi, and Russell Kahn. *145 Things to Be When You Grow Up: Planning a Successful Career While You're Still in High School.* New York, NY: Princeton Review Publishing, 2004.

bibliography

Alyeska Pipeline Service Company. "Pipeline Facts." May 8, 2008. Retrieved August 19, 2009 (http://www.alyeska-pipe. com/Pipelinefacts/PipelineConstruction.html).

Cornell, Casey. Interview with author, August 16, 2009.

Faloon, Kelly, and Katie Rotella. "Women in Plumbing: Where Are They? The Plumbing Industry Is Experiencing a Labor Shortage. So Why Not Hire Women?" *Plumbing & Mechanical*, November 1, 2002. Retrieved August 20, 2009 (http://www.accessmylibrary.com/coms2/ summary_0286-7886126_ITM).

Jackson, Albert. *Popular Mechanics Plumbing and Heating.* New York, NY: Hearst, 2006.

Levine, Wendy. "Women in the Plumbing Industry." *Reeves Journal*, March 12, 2008. Retrieved August 20, 2009 (http://www.reevesjournal.com/ Articles/Feature_Article/BNP_GUID_9-5-2006_ A_10000000000000283427).

National Association of Home Builders. *Build a Career in the Building Industry.* Washington, DC: Home Builders Institute, 2007.

Rich, Jason. 202 *High-Paying Jobs You Can Land Without a College Degree.* Irvine, CA: Entrepreneur Press, 2006.

Richardson, John H. "The Tao of Plumbing: No Pipes, No Civilization." *Esquire*, August 2009, pp. 83–86.

Strauss, Robert. "Repairman's Advantage: Even in Hard Times, Things Need to Be Fixed." *New York Times*, August 5, 2009. Retrieved August 11, 2009 (http:// www.nytimes.com/2009/08/06/business/ smallbusiness/06sbiz.html).

Sumichrast, Michael, and David Davitaia. *Opportunities in Building Construction Careers*. New York, NY: McGraw-Hill, 2008.

U.S. Department of Labor, Bureau of Labor Statistics. *The Big Book of Jobs*, 2007–2008 ed. New York, NY: McGraw-Hill, 2007.

Washington, DC Plumbers Local 5. "How to Be a Successful Apprentice." October 3, 2007. Retrieved August 20, 2009 (http://www.local5plumbers.org/viewarticle.asp?a=1941).

Woodson, R. Dodge. *Plumber's Licensing Study Guide*. 2nd ed. New York, NY: McGraw-Hill, 2007.

index

A

appliance installation, 12, 39
apprenticeships, 24, 27–29, 31,
    32–38, 52, 58, 65
associate's degree, 25
augers, 48

B

bachelor's degree, 25
blueprints, 25, 32, 35, 40

C

center punch, 45
chain-link cutters, 46
chemistry, 24
community college, 25, 27, 29, 30
connectors, 43
contractors, 8, 34
copper pipe, 51
couplings, 53
cross fittings, 53

D

demolition and cutting tools, 45–46
drafting, 24

E

elbow fittings, 53

F

files, 46
fire protection systems, 23
first aid, 35, 52
fittings, 53
fixture installation, 12

G

gas line installation, 12
gender discrimination, 64–65
General Educational
    Development (GED)
    diploma, 30, 34
gray water systems, 7, 63
green plumbing, 6, 59–63
guidance counselors, 29–30

H

hacksaws, 46
heatstroke, 52
high-efficiency fixtures, 59, 61

I

irrigation systems, 66–67

J

Job Corps, 30
journeypersons, 54–55, 65

L

licensing exams, 54, 57–59
low-flow toilets, 6, 59, 61

M

master plumbers, 32, 54, 55, 65
math skills, 24, 58
measuring tools, 45
mechanical drawing, 24
military training, 30–31

O

on-call work, 13, 22

P

physics, 24
pipe, types of, 50–53
pipe fitters, 8, 16–18, 20, 24,
     31, 52
pipe installation, 12, 39, 40–41,
     42–43
pipe layers, 8, 16, 18–20, 52
plumber, interview with a, 58–59
Plumbers Union Local 5, 37
plumbing
     career opportunities in, 8, 10–12,
          65–67
     education for, 24–31
     job outlook for, 5¬–7, 59, 67
     job responsibilities in, 5, 39–40
     licensing and, 31, 54–59
     on-the-job safety and, 15, 25,
          34, 48, 52

tools used in, 45–48
     women in the industry, 63–65
     work environment in, 12–15
plumbing assistant, 13
plumbing codes, 7, 25, 30, 56, 57
plumbing estimators, 65
plumbing inspector, 65
plumbing job, step-by-step overview
     of a, 40–43
plungers, 48
PolyPipe, 51
PVC, 51

R

radiant heating systems, 60,
     61–62

S

safety tools, 48
shock, 52
solar heating systems, 60, 61
soldering irons, 46
sprinkler fitters, 8, 16, 23
steamfitters, 8, 16, 20–22

T

technical schools, 25, 27
tees, 53
tin snips, 45
torches, 46
Trans-Alaska Pipeline System, 20
traps, 43
tubing cutters, 46

U

unions, 10, 13, 34, 36, 37
United Association of Journeymen
    and Apprentices of the
    Plumbing and Pipe Fitting
    Industry of the United States
    and Canada, 10, 36
U.S. Bureau of Labor Statistics,
    8, 10
U.S. Department of Labor, 30

V

vents, 43
vocational schools, 24, 25, 27, 30,
    58, 60

W

wages, 37
wire cutters, 46
wrenches, 46

ABOUT THE AUTHOR

Simone Payment has a degree in psychology from Cornell University and a master's degree in elementary education from Wheelock College. She is the author of twenty-three books for young adults. Her book *Inside Special Operations: Navy SEALs* (also from Rosen Publishing) won a 2004 Quick Picks for Reluctant Young Adult Readers award from the American Library Association and is on the Nonfiction Honor List of Voice of Youth Advocates.

PHOTO CREDITS

Cover, p. 1 (background) © www.istockphoto.com/christian Lagereek; cover, p. 1 (inset) © www.istockphoto.com/DIGIcal; p. 4 © www.istockphoto.com/Mike Clarke; p. 9 © Sonda Dawes/The Image Works; p. 11 © David Bacon/The Image Works; pp. 14–15 © Eduardo Contreras/San Diego Union-Tribune/Zuma Press; pp. 16–17, 44, 49 Shutterstock.com; pp. 18–19, 47 © Howard Lipin/San Diego Union-Tribune/Zuma Press; p. 21 SuperStock/Getty Images; pp. 22–23 © Carl J. Single/Syracuse Newspapers/The Image Works; p. 26 © Michael Sofronski/The Image Works; pp. 28–29 © James Marshall/The Image Works; p. 33 © Scott Keeler/St. Petersburg Times/Zuma Press; p. 34, 50–51, 56–57 © AP Images; p. 36 © Dick Schmidt/The Sacramento Bee/Zuma Press; pp. 40–41 © Jim Baird/San Diego Union-Tribune/Zuma Press; p. 42 © www.istockphoto.com/Ana Abejon; pp. 54–55 Ann Hermes/The Christian Science Monitor/Getty Images; pp. 60–61 Ian Waldie/Getty Images; pp. 62–63 Image Source/Getty Images; pp. 66–67 © Keith Beaty/The Toronto Star/Zuma Press.

Designer: Matt Cauli; Photo Researcher: Amy Feinberg